Why Is It Dark?

A **Just Ask** Book

by Chris Arvetis
and Carole Palmer

illustrated by James Buckley

Printed in the United States of America
by Rand McNally & Company
Library of Congress Catalog Card Number: 84-60770
First Printing, 1984

CHILDRENS PRESS CHOICE
A Rand McNally title selected for educational distribution

ISBN 0-516-09805-5

1984 SCHOOL AND LIBRARY EDITION

We have to stop.
It's getting too dark
to play.

It is getting dark!

Every day it gets dark.
I wonder why?

Each day the sun seems to
disappear from the sky.
Let's go see Mrs. Owl.
Maybe she can tell us why!

Mrs. Owl
will know!
She is
smart!

Can you tell us,
Mrs. Owl, why
it gets dark?

I want to know too!

Why yes,
I think I can.

First of all, we live on the earth.
The earth is a PLANET.
Say it with me–
PLAN–ET.

PLAN–ET!

PLAN–ET!
PLAN–ET!

The planet earth goes
around the sun.
The path the earth takes
is called its ORBIT.
Can you say that ?
OR–BIT !

OR–BIT !

Let me show you.
We'll use a ball
for the planet earth
and we'll pretend the
flashlight is the sun.

Interesting!

Hmmm!

You take the earth.
Start here and walk
around the sun.
Make a big path.

Go all the way around.
It takes the earth
about 365 days to
go around the sun.
That's one year.

Follow the path!

365 days!
That is one year!

But that's only part of it.
The earth also turns,
or ROTATES, like a top
as it goes around the sun.
It takes 24 hours for the
earth to turn around once.
Let me show you.

The X marks where we live
on the earth.
The flashlight is the sun
shining on the earth.
When the sun is shining
on that side of the earth
where the X is, it is daytime.

It is light
on this side!

As the earth turns,
that part faces away
from the sun.
Then it is nighttime
where we live—
and it is dark!

It is dark on this side!
Fascinating!

Or, to look at it another way, just imagine this...
When it is daytime where Christopher lives, it is dark on the other side of the world, where another mouse will be fast asleep.

And 12 hours later it will be the other way around!
I get it!

Let's look at the sun
and the earth again.
This little ball is the moon.
Just as the earth orbits
the sun, the moon goes
around the earth.

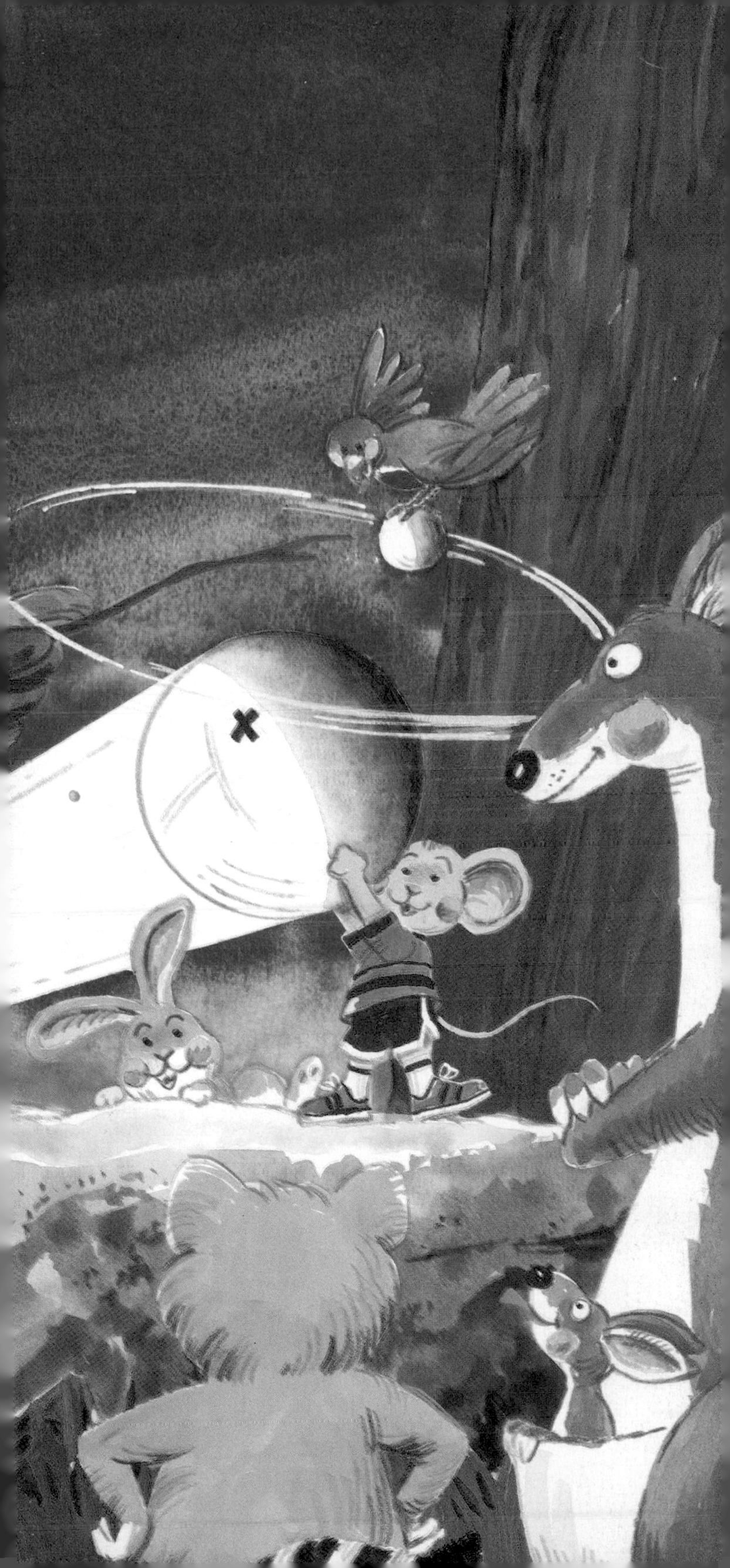

Look at my picture.
The sun's light shines on the earth and the moon.
Then the sunlight REFLECTS, or bounces off, the moon.

Did you know that?
Did you?

We see
the bright moon
in the sky, so it is
a lot less dark
even though it
is night.

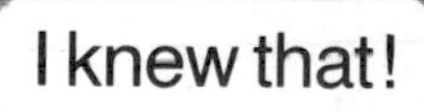
I knew that!

Just remember–
The earth goes around the sun.
When our part of the earth
faces the sun, it is day.
When it faces away
from the sun, it is night.
And it is dark.

The earth is turning all the time!
Wow!

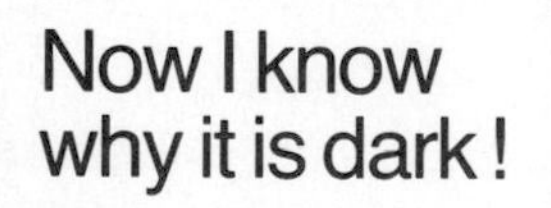
Now I know
why it is dark!
We do too
Me too!